Discover
North Cornwall

Paul White

Bossiney Books

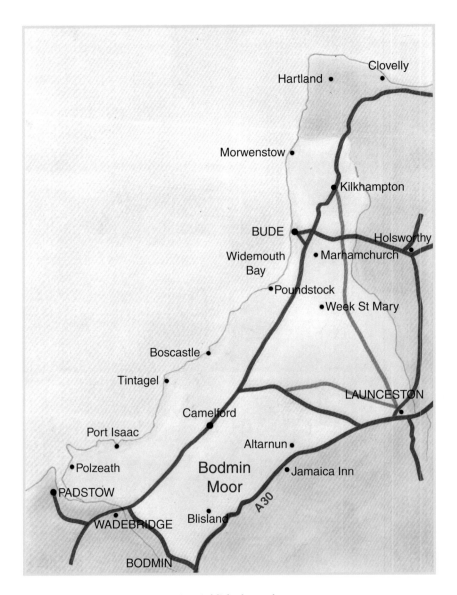

First published 2019 by
Bossiney Books Ltd, 67 West Busk Lane, Otley, LS21 3LY
www.bossineybooks.com

ISBN 978-1-906474-82-9

Acknowledgements

The maps are by Graham Hallowell. All photographs are by the author.

Printed in Great Britain by R Booth Ltd, Penryn, Cornwall

Introduction

The character of North Cornwall

Firstly, how do we define North Cornwall? There have been various administrative definitions over the years, but for the purpose of this book we mean the whole of the county north of the A30 and the River Camel, so excluding Bodmin, Wadebridge and Padstow. However, anyone visiting the western part of the area should certainly take in Padstow, perhaps by ferry from Rock.

Cornwall is famous for its coast, with stunning cliff scenery and a range of coves and beaches, and North Cornwall has that in abundance, but inland it differs from the rest of the county in being much less densely populated. Historically it was an area of isolated small farms which pastured cattle, goats and sheep: Launceston was the only substantial town.

The reason is geological: the north does not have the proliferation of mineral resources which is to be found in the rest of the county on the edge of the granite outcrops. There was some medieval tin-streaming on the edge of Bodmin Moor, and a scattering of small exploratory mines at later periods but these were never very profitable and there is little to see now. There is nothing to compare with West Cornwall or with the Minions area in the southern half of Bodmin Moor, areas where the miners struck lucky.

On the other hand, there is abundant evidence of quarrying for slate around Tintagel and especially at Delabole, where the quarry has been operating since the 15th century if not earlier; there are granite quarries near St Breward and there was until 2002 a china clay works all too near to Rough Tor – but it was nowhere near the scale of the china clay area north of St Austell.

None of these extractive industries ever needed the size of labour force typical of the mining areas, nor did related engineering industries develop as they did in West Cornwall.

A further reason for this was inaccessibility. Before 1800, North Cornwall's 'roads' were no better than muddy bridleways. Transport was by packhorses, taking products to the coast for shipment

A former slate quarry near Tintagel

The centre of Stratton, a small town on the outskirts of Bude. It was once a much larger and more significant place than Bude

– but North Cornwall lacked good harbours. Some slate was carried to Boscastle but, because of transport costs, slate from other areas, especially North Wales, easily undercut the price of North Cornwall's slate everywhere except locally.

West Cornwall had its first horse-drawn railway, leading from a mine to a port, by 1812, and steam locomotives almost as soon as they were invented. In North Cornwall by contrast, Camelford wasn't connected to the rail network until 1892, Wadebridge until 1895 and Bude until 1898. Bude developed rapidly as a seaside resort, but it was alone. And all of North Cornwall's railways had disappeared by 1967.

It is this quiet history which gives North Cornwall much of its charm: a coastline with relatively little modern development, except at Bude and Polzeath, and inland a large number of tranquil and attractive villages – in one of which I lived for many years.

Place names and what they reveal

North Cornwall used to be administratively divided into three 'hundreds': from north to south, Stratton, Lesnewth and Trigg. When place name elements like Tre- or -ton (which meant nearly the same thing in Cornish and Anglo-Saxon) are plotted on a map, a very clear boundary line emerges along the River Ottery, which passes through Canworthy Water, with Tre- to the south and -ton to the north. The same applies with Cornish Bos- and Saxon -cot or -worthy. Historians believe this means that the hundred of Stratton was Saxon-speaking from the 8th century – but it was still accepted by the Saxon kingdom of Wessex, and later by England, as part of a semi-independent Cornwall.

Of course, the language people speak is not a genetic identifier, and many countries (such as Wales or Belgium) have more than one language, with a geographical division between them, but this is an interesting historical clue nonetheless.

North Cornwall and Devon merge seamlessly: the River Tamar has never been the absolute eastern boundary. An area west of the Tamar but north of the Ottery was part of Devon until 1966. There are still three anomalies, which exist in order to keep the whole of each parish in a single county – North Tamerton within Cornwall, Bridgerule and Pancrasweek within Devon.

Beaches and walks

This book does not pretend to be a beach and cove guide. There is a useful website, www.cornwall-beaches.co.uk or see *Cornwall – the Beach & Cove Guide* published by Tor Mark.

For walks, please see other Bossiney books:

Really Short Walks – North Cornwall (3-6km walks)
Shortish Walks – North Cornwall (6-8km walks)
Shortish Walks – Bodmin Moor (6-8km walks)

The towns

Launceston

Launceston has probably the most interesting town centre in Cornwall: if it were in Tuscany, English tourists would make a bee-line for this hill-town, rather than rushing past on the A30 as they mostly do. Launceston is a successful town, well positioned beside the A30 and with three industrial estates, but its distinctive geography has preserved the town centre intact. The mix of medieval town and castle walls and gateways, narrow streets and elegant Georgian houses is well worth exploring. See page 36 for a town centre walk, together with a slightly longer walk to explore the outlying areas of St Stephens and Newport.

The castle (above) was built by William the Conqueror's half-brother and is mentioned in Domesday Book (1087) so it must have been started very soon after the conquest in 1066, and reached its peak in the 13th century. It is maintained by English Heritage and it can be visited, though you can get a good view of it for free.

The old name of the settlement on the north side of the Kensey valley was Lan-Stefan, meaning 'churchyard of Stephen'. (The settlement on the south side was originally called Dunheved.) The Saxons made it Lan-Stephan-tun. By corruption it became Launceston, now pronounced 'Launston' by outsiders, 'Launs'n' or 'Laans'n' by locals.

Probably on account of its position so near the Cornish border, and therefore convenient for rulers based in England, Launceston was the County Town until 1835, when the much more central Bodmin replaced it once the roads had been improved. Today Truro is the county town.

Within the town the attractions include the castle (English Heritage, entry charge) and the Lawrence House Museum (seasonal opening, free) in a beautiful Georgian town house, which concentrates on local history, but also has a collection of costumes.

The church of St Mary Magdalene has an extraordinary exterior of carved granite and there is a recumbent statue of St Mary at the east end.

Inside there is a pre-Reformation pulpit.

In the valley between the hills you will find the Launceston Steam Railway, a narrow-gauge heritage line run by enthusiasts and working in the tourist season.

Left: The Launceston Steam Railway

Opposite, top: Summerleaze, one of Bude's beaches

Opposite, lower: the Bude Canal

Bude

Bude began to develop as a town in the early nineteenth century: until then Stratton, now more like a village, was more significant.

It was the opening of the Bude Canal in 1823 which began the change. The canal was unusual in several ways. It was built to carry sand inland from Bude beach: the sand is rich in lime and was invaluable as a fertiliser for the acid soils of the inland farms, but the canal was also useful for carrying coal inland. Because of a poor water supply, even after the formation of the Lower Tamar Lake, it was designed with inclined planes rather than locks; there were six planes in all, one as steep as 1 in 4, with rails. Tub boats with wheels were used instead of barges. The canal stretched nearly to Launceston, with a branch to Holsworthy and another up to Lower Tamar Lake, 57km (35 1/2 miles) in all.

The canal builders also made major improvements to Bude harbour. The first two miles of canal, to Helebridge, were built as a broad canal with a sea lock and a new breakwater. This enabled sea-going ships to moor safely, and off-load into the tubs; trade developed. By the mid-century, Bude's population contained many 'master mariners' – captains of small coasting vessels.

Seaside towns were developing rapidly in the Victorian period, and Bude wanted to become one. By 1871 there was a hotel and a range of lodging houses, but the town was relatively difficult to access, until in 1879 the railway reached Holsworthy. A 'luxury

coach service' was provided from there to Bude. The town's population doubled between 1881 and 1911. It would not be until 1898 that the railway reached Bude, and it closed in 1966 by which time road transport had made it unnecessary.

The town is fortunate in having an excellent local museum, the Bude Heritage Centre, with free entry at the time of writing. It is housed in Bude Castle (photo above), which is a gentleman's house built in 1830 with castellations. Its original owner was Sir Goldsworthy Gurney, and he may have been responsible for the castle's innovative use of a concrete raft for its foundations.

Sir Goldsworthy Gurney (1793-1875) was a remarkable man. Born near Padstow, he became a practising surgeon but achieved fame as a scientist and inventor. His most lasting contribution was probably the oxy-hydrogen blowpipe which produced a controllable flame of great brilliancy, and which he developed in the 'Bude-Light', an extremely bright oil lamp which was used to light the House of Commons. Further inventions in ventilating both buildings and mines were also successes.

Perhaps he is now most remembered for an invention which never made it – a steam road vehicle which was based on the ideas of Richard Trevithick. Gurney was working on this in 1825 and his carriage made a trip from London to Bath and back in 1829 travelling at 20 mph. A regular service was briefly established to Cheltenham, but there was strong opposition, both from ordinary people understandably scared of possible boiler explosions and from the established horse-drawn transport industry. Suddenly more than fifty private Acts of Parliament imposed tolls on steam vehicles ten times as high as those on stage coaches. Gurney was

Camelford Town Hall, built in 1806, now the Library

bankrupted. Meanwhile steam railways expanded rapidly, and soon made long distance road transport look obsolescent.

Camelford

This is a small town which grew because it was on the main Falmouth to London road. In 1675 John Ogilby's route map said:

> Cambleford, seated on the Camel, is a small town
> scarce numbering 50 houses, in the parish of Lanicolas
> [Lanteglos] a mile distant, yet sends burgesses to
> Parliament, and is governed by a Mayor, Recorder and
> 8 magistrates; has a small market on Fridays and 3 fairs
> yearly, the 15th May, the 7th of July and St John's in August,
> having some inns affording good accommodation.

The town lost its MPs in 1832. Whilst Camelford is not unattractive, there is little to explore. The A39 still runs through the old centre, sometimes causing traffic delays.

The North Cornwall Museum is a privately owned museum concentrating on early twentieth century life.

The stroll out from Morwenstow church car park is nearly flat, but takes you to these stunning views, to the north (left) and down to the rocks (right). The coast path itself is very far from flat!

North of Bude

Cornwall's most northerly parish is **Morwenstow**, once home to the famously eccentric vicar, Revd Robert Stephen Hawker, who is remembered for writing Cornwall's anthem, 'The Song of the Western Men' (And shall Trelawney die? Here's twenty thousand Cornish men Will know the reason why) and for the innovation of harvest festivals – but his life and eccentricities are worth investigating.

For visitors, the main area to visit is Crosstown, with its characterful pub the Bush Inn, beyond which are the parish church and rectory and the Rectory Farm Tearooms, the ideal place for a lunch or a cream tea. There are excellent walks from here, though some of the cliff paths are very steep.

However, the stroll from the church car park out to the cliffs is easy, and you can visit Hawker's Hut, the National Trust's smallest property. Hawker used to sit here smoking opium and contemplating the sea.

If returning southward, you may wish to divert right (COOMBE VALLEY) passing the GCHQ listening station, with its huge satellite receivers. Duckpool beach at the seaward end of the valley is attractive and usually uncrowded, not least because swimming here is unsafe.

From Duckpool, go inland to Stibb. From there you can go either to **Kilkhampton**, with its impressive church and its motte-and-bailey castle about 1 km (half a mile) west of the village; or you can head south to **Poughill** (pronounced 'Puffill') which has an ancient church with frescoes, fifteenth century but enthusiastically repainted by Frank Salisbury (1874-1962).

Above: Upper Tamar Lake, has an easy walk around it

Below: The Lower Tamar Lake is excellent for bird-watching, though I was particularly lucky to spot this juvenile sparrowhawk

On the Devon border east of Kilkhampton lie the Tamar Lakes, which are full of leisure possibilities. The Upper Tamar Lake has an activity centre offering kayaking, sailing and windsurfing, with tuition. Coarse fishing permits are available. There is an accessible 5 km (3 mile) walk right round the lake. Both lakes have bird hides, and whilst they do have an interconnecting woodland path they each have their own car park.

The Lower Tamar Lake is smaller and managed as a nature reserve. Whereas the Upper Lake was formed as a reservoir for the surrounding area, the Lower Lake was formed in the 1820s to collect water to supply the Bude Canal: the Bude Aqueduct Trail makes a flat and attractive stroll for whatever distance you choose.

Widemouth Bay from the south

Bude to Boscastle

A little south of Bude is **Widemouth Bay**, with a fine beach 2 km (1 1/2 miles) long. It has facilities for learning surfing. At low tide there is an expanse of rock pools. At either end there are free car parks, which are popular with people who want to sit in their car and observe the majesty of the ocean – just the place to eat your lunchtime sandwich!

The next cove southward from Widemouth is at Millook, which is a must for anyone interested in geology – it was voted one of Britain's best sites for 'folding and faulting' by the Geological Society of London – but parking is extremely limited. And in no circumstances try driving north from Millook towards Bude as it is probably the steepest hill in England, and single track; if you meet something coming the other way, a hill-start may be impossible.

Inland from Millook, but not directly accessible from there, is **Poundstock**, where the church is beautifully situated, with its early 16th century 'Gildhall' (or church house) nearby. The church has interesting features including wall paintings as well as part of the original rood screen.

Above: Poundstock church and Gildhall
Below: Crackington Haven

The next beach with a car park and facilities for visitors is at **Crackington Haven**, with its dramatic cliffs: the highest cliff in England, High Cliff, is just over a mile south of the Haven. A little to the north is the hamlet of St Gennys and the parish church, in part Norman.

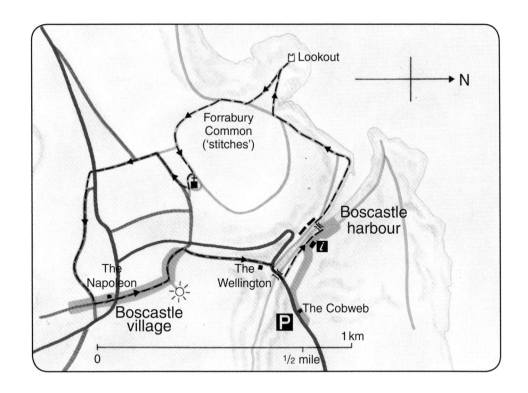

Boscastle and Tintagel

These are the two 'must-see' places on the North Cornwall coast, both of them the result of extreme geology. At Boscastle, a particularly hard lump of rock prevented the river running straight out to sea: instead it forced a circuitous route which created a natural harbour – though one demanding great skill to enter or leave in a sailing craft. The first mention of the harbour is in 1547, but it had probably been used for many centuries before that, if only for fishing.

'Boscastle' is a corruption of 'Botreaux Castle', and the motte of the Norman castle still exists. The layout of the village is quite complex, as you can see from the map, which shows a walking route (4 km, 2 1/2 miles), full instructions for which can be found in *Really Short Walks: North Cornwall*. The layout is made even more complicated by the B3266 and New Road, which only date from the heyday of the port in the early 19th century, zigzagging across the old main street.

Boscastle harbour entrance, seen from Willa Park

In 1204 William de Botterell was granted the right to hold a market, and at about the same time created a small planned town running south, steeply uphill, from his castle. The site of the weekly market, which ceased in 1810, is now occupied by the Bottreaux Surgery. Some of the buildings in Fore Street and its continuation High Street are in part sixteenth century, and there has been little recent building there so it's very picturesque.

Forrabury Stitches, just beyond St Symphorian's church, are a rare surviving example of medieval strip farming, and out on the headland is a white lookout tower, built for private use as a summer house but later serving the coastguard and now the National Coastwatch.

Before the coming of the railways, which reached Launceston in 1865 but Camelford not until 1893, Boscastle was an important port for inland north Cornwall, importing coal from Wales and 'Bristol goods', which meant all kinds of things which Bristol had imported from around the world. The main exports were slate

The harbour seen from Penally Point, the rock at the seaward end

Looking in the opposite direction. The terrace of cottages on the right were originally the homes of fishermen, and the building behind them was a 'fish palace' where the catches were salted and nets mended

from Delabole and other local quarries, and also manganese, one of the few minerals mined in north Cornwall. It was used in bleaching cloth, so most of it went from Boscastle to Liverpool for the Lancashire mills, but it was also used in glassmaking. Surprisingly, there was a shipbuilding yard within the harbour.

In the early Victorian period there was serious rivalry between two Boscastle firms, those of Thomas Avery and Rosevear & Sloggatt. Both owned ships, as well as slate quarries, and their

Left: Forrabury stitches, a rare surviving example of medieval strip farming

Opposite: cottages in the upper village, probably sixteenth century in origin, if not earlier

inland activities extended from Bude to Padstow. Avery has left a reputation as 'a notorious wrecker', but he did not steal cargoes: he was simply usually the first on the scene and got the captain's permission to unload, store, and later sell the cargo on the owner's behalf. Rosevear & Sloggatt were furious, believing that as Lloyds Agents they should have the monopoly. The local magistrates backed Avery, the London courts (much nearer to Lloyds!) ruled against him.

From 1860 everything went wrong for Boscastle as a port. The sea trade declined, Cornish manganese was uneconomic compared to imports, the slate trade preferred Port Gaverne, the harbour's limekiln and malthouse both closed. Even the pilchards deserted the Cornish coast.

Fortunately tourism came to the rescue. It had started by the 1840s: houses, and later industrial buildings, were turned into lodgings, the Joiners Arms had been converted into the Wellington Hotel by 1860. The National Trust bought the harbour and the coastline in the 1950s. The village never looked back – except when hit by floods – the famous flood of 2004 was by no means the first. It destroyed many of the buildings, now faithfully replaced, but remarkably, despite the floodwater sweeping all the cars from the car park no lives were lost.

The Museum of Witchcraft and Magic has been in Boscastle since 1960, featuring folk magic as well as Wicca, and even Free-masonry. See page 40.

If you drive from Boscastle to Tintagel you will, after passing through Trethevy, descend steeply into Rocky Valley. There is limited parking on the left, and on the right a very scenic footpath winds out along the valley to the sea. On the way you pass the ruins of a mill, and on the cliff behind the mill there is a rock carving, which looks Bronze Age but is quite possibly the work of a bored but knowledgeable miller! At the end of the valley (photo below) it is possible to climb footpaths on either side for splendid coastal views, but they are very steep.

South of Bossiney lies **Tintagel**, a village which might be said to exist as the result of two authors. The first was Geoffrey of Monmouth who wrote, around 1136, *The History of the Kings of the Britons*, a large part of which is devoted to King Arthur. It is utterly unreliable as history, but was immensely successful in its day. This was before the invention of printing, but 215 manuscript copies survive – which compares with just 49 printed Gutenberg bibles.

According to Geoffrey, Arthur was conceived at Tintagel when his mother failed to notice that it was King Uther rather than her husband who had entered her bedroom. (A translation of this tabloid story appears in the present author's *King Arthur – Man or Myth*.) Geoffrey never claims Arthur was born here.

According to Geoffrey, King Arthur conquered or otherwise subdued most of western Europe. The Normans loved that idea, and identified themselves as Arthur's natural successors. Richard Earl of Cornwall, brother of Henry III, swapped property with Gervase de Tintagel and built himself a castle around AD 1230 to associate himself with Cornwall's folk hero, Arthur. It had no military purpose, and would gradually fall into the romantic decay we now see.

To a large extent the legend of King Arthur also fell into decay – until Alfred, Lord Tennyson started publishing *Idylls of the King*, starting in 1859 and continuing to 1885. This series of narrative poems was an immediate success, giving a new (and very Victorian) moral significance to the legends surrounding the Arthur story. Tourism to Cornwall was not new – Charles Dickens visited Tintagel in 1842 – but *Idylls of the King* greatly increased the number of people wanting to see Tintagel. And before long new railways made it much easier. Camelford station opened in 1893 and a horse bus took passengers to Tintagel, which caused huge changes locally, not least to the name.

'Tintagel' was the name of the parish, and of the castle, but the village which we now call Tintagel was officially 'Trevena' as late as 1901. Late Victorian tourists wanted to see *Tintagel*, and before long it *was* Tintagel. There were concerns about the speed and nature of other changes tourism brought: the first purchase of land anywhere in England by the National Trust was 14 acres of cliff at Tintagel's Barras Head in 1902, a response to the opening in 1899 of King Arthur's Castle Hotel, now called the Camelot Castle Hotel.

Old buildings in Trevena were soon being knocked down or converted into lodging houses or hotels, and the Old Post Office was acquired by the Trust in 1903. This medieval manor house, which was built as a farm around 1380, is one of the Trust's most fascinating properties (entrance charge).

Above: the Old Post Office   Below: the castle

Whilst it is possible to approach the castle on foot directly from the village, my own preference is to drive out to the car park just beyond the interesting Norman church of St Materiana. A short walk from the church gives a spectacular view of the island, the remains of the castle, and the cliffs.

Another building in the village which is well worth seeing is King Arthur's Great Halls (entrance charge). The exterior is a mid-Victorian house which gives no idea of what lies behind: it was extended in the early 1930s by Frederick Glasscock, a retired custard manufacturer who was obsessed with King Arthur. The extension is an astonishing piece of 1930s design, with its highlight a series of splendid stained glass windows by Veronica Whall

Archaeological work on the island since the late 1980s, and still continuing, has demonstrated that in the post-Roman period, say AD 400-750, the island was a seasonal home presumably for the kings of Dumnonia, fortified, with perhaps a hundred buildings, and with an access to Mediterranean trade unparalleled in the rest of Britain. The owners dined on local oysters, cod and roast pork, but ate from bowls made in Turkey and drank imported fine wines from glasses made in Spain. And among the archaeological finds there have been inscribed stones, with both Latin and Greek script. Perhaps King Arthur really did spend his summers here…

The coast south from Tintagel

A mile and a half (2 km) south from Tintagel lies **Trebarwith Strand**, accessible along the cliffs by the coast path – beautiful but with a very steep descent to Trebarwith. There's road access too! It's a great place for rockpooling and exploring caves when the tide is low, but beware getting cut off when it returns. The Port William pub has a superb location with outside seating.

The main route along the coast is the B3314, which passes through **Delabole**, where the huge slate quarry has been worked for at least 500 years. There are tours every weekday afternoon in summer. Further down the coast is the very attractive fishing village of **Port Isaac**, which some visitors will recognise as the location of the TV series *Doc Martin*. There is a car park at the top of the village, off the road to the little cove of Port Gaverne. Driving through the main part of the village is not recommended, and there is a footpath from the car park.

Further west still is the peaceful cove of **Port Quin**, a fishing hamlet which was also a small trading harbour in the medieval period. The decline of the population sparked an explanatory legend, that all the men of the village went to sea on a Sunday (wicked) and were all lost in a storm.

Above: a gull's eye view of Port Isaac

Opposite left: looking over Trebarwith Strand

The westward trend of the coastline after Port Quin ends abruptly at Pentire Point, where a short stroll out to the scenic headland The Rumps is possible from the car park at Pentire Farm (SW 936802).

Below: Port Quin

Above: Polzeath beach, popular for surfing and for families

Left: Daymer Bay beach, quieter because it's too sheltered for surfing

After that the coast turns south, to the first real beach resort since Widemouth Bay, at **Polzeath**. The beach here is popular both for surfing and for families.

A little further on there is an even larger beach at **Daymer Bay**, backed by sand dunes: it's quieter and also more sheltered than Polzeath.

On the coast path along the dunes between Daymer Bay and Rock, with Padstow in the distance

A short walk from the Daymer Bay car park takes you to St Enedoc's church, famous as the burial place of the popular poet Sir John Betjeman. It was once more famous for being swamped by sand: until 1863 the vicar and parishioners descended through the roof once a year for a service, which was obligatory if the vicar was to receive the tithes. It is surrounded by a golf course.

Further south is **Rock**, which has the highest proportion of second homes in Cornwall and is famously a place for the affluent, sometimes referred to as Chelsea-on-Sea. Watersports are very well catered for, and there are up-market pubs and restaurants with outdoor terraces.

Should you need to arrive in Rock by private helicopter, consult http://www.rockpad.co.uk

One great attraction of Rock is the pedestrian (and cycle) ferry across to Padstow, which has been operating since 1337. There is a car park very near the ferry landing point.

*The pedestrian ferry
arriving at Rock
from Padstow*

Padstow

This is a very ancient place, named after the 6th century St Petroc. It still has an active fishing harbour. By Tudor times, and into the 18th century, it was a significant port for trade with Ireland, though access to the harbour was always made difficult by the sandbank Doom Bar, on which many ships were stranded. Today the town is famous among foodies for its restaurants. Both the harbour and the streets are not to be missed, and there are pleasant walks along the coast.

Altarnun

Bodmin Moor

The moor is in many ways like Dartmoor, much of it apparently wild and unsuitable for agriculture. In fact Dartmoor, Bodmin Moor, the St Austell area, West Penwith and the Isles of Scilly are all outcrops of what geologists call the 'Cornubian batholith' – a mass of granite running along the spine of the peninsula.

The moor was not always so deserted: in the second millenium BC the climate was better and subsistence farming was possible. Much evidence of the period is still visible. Again in the Middle Ages, the 13th century AD in particular, an expanding population farmed it extensively, till the Black Death reduced population pressure. There are abandoned medieval settlements and field systems.

So there is much to explore on foot on Bodmin Moor, but be sure to take care – there are some seriously boggy areas. You will need an OS map and a compass as well as walking gear. Both *Really Short Walks – North Cornwall* and *Shortish Walks – Bodmin Moor* offer some safe options. For this book we suggest a short tour by car, taking in some attractive villages, stone circles and other features.

Left: Temple church
Right: Burnard's bust of John Wesley at Altarnun

Start at **Altarnun**, a village 13 km (8 miles) west of Launceston. The church is very impressive, with a rood screen, a Norman font and a fine set of carved bench ends. Not far from the church is St Nonna's Holy Well, once used for 'bowsening' – throwing a supposed 'lunatic' backwards into the water so that they would be cured by the shock. Whilst useless for the patient, perhaps it relieved the frustrations of uncomprehending relatives.

Across the stream a street of attractive stone cottages rises towards the main road at Five Lanes, passing a Methodist chapel with a bust of John Wesley above the door – the work of Neville Northey Burnard at the age of only sixteen. Burnard (1818-1878) was the son of an Altarnun stone-mason but became a highly successful sculptor, even commissioned by Queen Victoria. After the death of a daughter he took to drink, became a tramp and died in Redruth workhouse.

From Five Lanes, a short diversion to the right on the old road brings you to **Trewint**, where Wesley Cottage (open in summer Tuesday-Thursday) is a small Wesley museum. Wesley used to stay there on his numerous visits to Cornwall. Here is an entry from his journal for 2 April 1744:

> I preached at five and rode on toward Launceston. The
> hills were covered with snow, as in the depth of winter.
> About two we came to Trewint, wet and weary enough,

having been battered by the rain and hail for some hours. I preached in the evening to many more than the house would contain, on the happiness of him whose sins are forgiven. In the morning Diggory Isbel undertook to pilot us over the great moor, all the paths being covered in snow which, in many places, was driven together, too deep for horse or man to pass. The hail followed us for the first seven miles; we had then a fair, though exceeding sharp, day. I preached at Gwennap in the evening…

Return to Five Lanes and join the A30 in the direction of Bodmin. After 5km (3 miles) take the exit to Bolventor and **Jamaica Inn**. The inn dates from 1750, nearly 20 years before the road was turn-piked. Sir William Trelawney who was Lord of the Manor was also governor of Jamaica. From 1880 until WW2 it was a temperance hotel. The inn was made famous by Daphne du Maurier's novel, and now has a museum of smuggling.

Continue past the inn on the old road, which soon rejoins the A30. Leave it at the second exit (TEMPLE) which again takes you on the old road. **Temple** was a hospice founded by the Knights Templars around AD 1120 and was notorious for being until 1744 a Cornish equivalent of Gretna Green: as Richard Carew put it, 'many a bad marriage bargain is there yearly slubbered up'. The church was rebuilt in 1883, but if you enjoy the simplicity of the old road, you will probably enjoy the church too: park just beyond the village war memorial and walk down to the left.

The next destination is **Blisland**. Continue on the old road through Temple, turn right signed BODMIN LAUNCESTON and cross the A30 on a bridge. Then follow the narrow lanes to Blisland, ignoring unmarked side turnings.

Blisland is unusual in Cornwall as a settlement surrounding a village green, and in the best village green tradition it has two excellent attractions, the pub and the church. The church is essentially Norman, but with an incongruous 17th century pulpit. However the *piéce de resistance* is the colourful rood screen, dating from 1896. Betjeman thought it nearly unique as a Victorian restoration project which actually improved the church.

The green at Blisland

Leave Blisland on the road signed for ST BREWARD, passing the Village Hall and following such signs as there are. You will cross the De Lank river at Delford Bridge, a spot popular for picnics and paddling.

St Breward's main industry has always been granite quarrying. Pass the church, heading north, take a right turn (unsigned), keep left at a fork (unsigned) and again at the next junction (unsigned). When you reach open downland, continue straight ahead, towards Roughtor on the horizon. This leads to a former china clay quarry, now converted to a reservoir, with its gate labelled 'Stannon House', where the maintained tarmac ends.

Park here and walk a further 250m (300 yards) and Stannon stone circle (SX126800) is a short distance to your right. It has no fewer than 47 stones still upright. There are two other stone circles within easy walking distance, Louden at SX132795 and Fernacre at SX145800.

Turn your car round and this time bear right, then take the first right (unsigned) to and through a hamlet. Cross a stream and immediately turn right (unsigned) and you will come to a cross-roads. You could turn right, which takes you to the Roughtor car park, from which there is a fine view and excellent walks.

Top: The Stannon stone circle
Below: Roughtor seen from the car park

Alternatively go straight on (DAVIDSTOW) which leads past the Crowdy reservoir and through Davidstow Woods to Davidstow Airfield. A left turn takes you to the A39.

A right turn, soon followed by a very sharp left turn, would take you to two museums, the Davidstow Moor RAF Memorial Museum (donations appreciated) and the Cornwall at War Museum (entry charge, limited opening, booking essential).

A walk round Launceston and St Stephens

The walk is about 5.5 km (3 1/2 miles) long and is in two parts: a very short walk around the town centre, then an exploration of the older settlement at St Stephens. The longer walk has one steep ascent and two steep descents.

The town centre walk

Start from the multi-storey car park in Westgate Street and walk past the Westgate Inn, then bear left to the town square. Notice the doorway of the White Hart Hotel: its stonework was recycled from an Augustinian Priory, founded in 1136. Keep right at the far end of the square, noticing the old bootmaker's sign above one of the shops.

Turn right into Southgate Street to take a look at the surviving town gateway. Seen from the other (outer) side, it made a grand entrance to the medieval walled town, and indeed to Cornwall, since many travellers arrived by way of Exeter Street, having crossed the Tamar at Polson Bridge.

Return along Southgate Street then continue ahead until you reach the church, St Mary Magdalene, which Nikolaus Pevsner described in *The Buildings of England: Cornwall* as 'the most spectacular church west of Exeter' though he says its amazing carved granite exterior is 'decorated with barbarous profuseness'. I fear he was giving marks for effort but not for style. Don't miss the recumbent statue outside at the east end.

The church dates from around 1520. Before that, Launceston only had a chapel, its mother church being St Stephens across the valley. Carry on past the church and keep left down to a street of elegant Georgian houses, a reminder that the Assizes and other county town functions sometimes brought grand personages to Launceston, and Cornwall accommodated them in style. (One of these houses is the Lawrence House Museum, free entry and well worth a visit, Mon-Fri 10.30-4.30.)

Turn left, and enter the bailey of the castle, passing the remains of 'Lanson gaol', a dungeon of fearsome reputation. Leave by the main gate, and the car park is all too clearly visible ahead of you.

Left: The market place   Right: The South Gate

The longer walk

Emerging from the castle gateway, turn left and follow the wall up. Take a left turn into an unpromising back street. When it swings left, take a narrow alley to the right.

When you reach a street turn left, then opposite the Methodist church, turn right then immediately left on a footpath which descends past the side of the Jobcentre. In earlier times, when there were no wheeled vehicles in Cornwall, this was the main road out of the town to the north. Walk down, crossing two streets.

On meeting a major road, cross with care to the pavement on the other side (and notice the narrow gauge Launceston Steam Railway below). Carry on down past the traffic lights, over the River Kensey and past the Gothick 'round house', with its explanatory plaque, to a mini-roundabout.

Continue up ST STEPHENS HILL, past very old cottages on the left. Pass the toll house and cross over to take a look at the church. (There is a weatherworn Norman carving on the outside east wall.)

The Saxons built St Stephens to a grid-plan, which you can still just about discern if you look hard. Continue on the Bude road for another 100m beyond the church, then turn left into NORTH STREET, which swings left and passes the front of the Golf Club. Turn right at the former elementary school, then left and left again at GALLOWS HILL – the traditional place of execution.

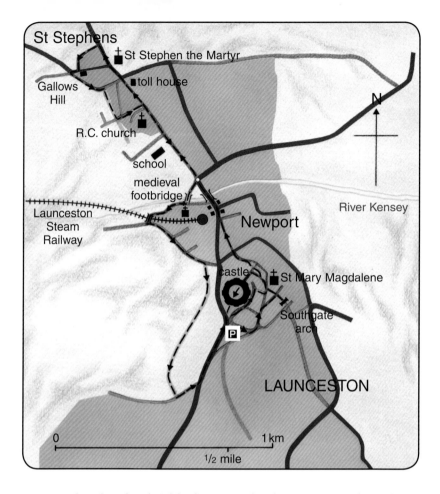

Immediately after 'Fielden' turn right down a green lane (part of the Saxon grid-plan) as far as a street. The green lane continues down, but there is no through route, so turn left along the street. Walk ahead into HOLLIES CLOSE and take the footway at the far end out to St Stephens Hill. Turn right, and return to the mini-roundabout.

Bear right along WESTBRIDGE ROAD and cross the river by a medieval footbridge leading to St Thomas's church. Behind the church once stood an Augustinian priory, of which very little remains.

Turn right at the church and follow the curving lane to cross the railway. Turn left at the T-junction.

Pass a terrace of cottages, then continue ahead at the junction. Follow a track to the right of FOUNDRY GARDENS. Pass two more

38

terraces then turn right on PUBLIC FOOTPATH. Follow the way-marked path, with its views of the castle towering above you.

On reaching a lane, turn left and climb to join the main road. Continue as far as the castle gate, then turn right to the car park.

More North Cornwall attractions

Tamar Otter and Wildlife Centre

Situated at North Petherwin, 8 km (5 miles) north-west of Launceston, this family-run 20 acre site is a fine place to see wildlife, not just otters but deer, wallabies, meercats, owls and other birds of prey. The staff give excellent talks and visitors can get really close to the animals – except the otters, which are liable to bite!

Museum of Witchcraft and Magic, Boscastle

This museum has 4000 objects reflecting both historic and contemporary forms of witchcraft. It's probably unsuitable for young children, as some exhibits are quite explicit, and it's certainly not a frivolous Halloween-style experience – indeed some visitors might find it heavy going; others will appreciate the informative detail.

Pencarrow House

A Georgian country house and gardens at the southern edge of our area. Guided tours of the house take about an hour.

Other Bossiney books you may find useful

About Tintagel
King Arthur – Man or Myth?
King Arthur's Footsteps
Really Short Walks – North Cornwall
Shortish Walks – North Cornwall
Shortish Walks – Bodmin Moor